pathetic:
essays on enumerated social failings

pathetic:
essays on enumerated social failings

shannon mcleod

etchings press
indianapolis

Copyright© 2016 by Shannon McLeod

This publication is made possible by the funding provided by the College of Arts and Sciences and the English Department at the University of Indianapolis. Special thanks to IngramSpark and to those students who judged, edited, designed, and published this chapbook: Mikaela Bielawski and Shannon Gaskin.

UNIVERSITY *of*
INDIANAPOLIS

Published by Etchings Press
1400 E. Hanna Ave.
Indianapolis, Indiana 46227

All rights reserved

etchings.uindy.edu
www.uindy.edu/cas/english

Printed by IngramSpark
ingramspark.com

Published in the United States of America

ISBN 978-0-9903475-3-8

23 22 21 20 19 18 17 16   2 3 4
Second Printing, 2019

table of contents

Six Years Ago	7
Learning to Tap Dance in Adulthood	9
Non-Refundable	13
Panty Display	19
Bad Thief	21
Bad Mentor	23
Goodbye Yellow Brick Road	27
Stranger Parts	31
My Hangover Cure is Your Hangover	33
Acknowledgements	35

The names of the individuals mentioned in the stories have been changed to protect the innocent.

six years ago

This jazz café is only open on Fridays. It is tightly packed with acquaintances. Even those you've never met before look familiar. And after a few drinks, it is not inappropriate to invite yourself to their tables to investigate social connections. Our stories are similar in this circle, which is why we stick together. This college boy, who is presently talking to you, has you stuck at a table that is shoved beside the corner where the musicians perform with an upright bass, a piano, a guitar, two singers—male and female— who trade off the microphone between songs when they aren't sharing it in a duet. Mounted on the burgundy walls are tarnished brass instruments and old records. The place is lit with lamps of vinyl, lace, and some Tiffany knock-offs. It reminds you of an eccentric great-aunt's house. The couches are even embroidered with flowers and topped with clear plastic slipcovers. And it smells like smoke and dust. The college boy is studying sculpture. He is exasperated with his life, he tells you, as though he is unaware of the strange and beautiful sanctuary he is sitting in. He complains that nobody gets it. Everyone is living a life that ignores beauty and shits on art. You simultaneously hate and pity him. He claims he is not enjoying a time he will soon idealize. You drink your gin and tonic. (You never know what else to order.) He pulls out a cigarette, and you imagine what his life will be like in six years. He does not know it yet, but he will resent his family and his job because they will keep him from evenings like this—feeling bored in a sea of friends while musicians, who play for fun, not money, are goofing through a piano cover of a Sublime song. Jesus Christ, this is tiring, entertaining his boredom, nodding at how the world has already disappointed him before the age of twenty-two. He will remember this night and the slew of nights like it. He will think about it longingly. He will misremember, though, recalling dancing along to the music, when he really just hunched over his phone and forced strangers into his conversation. You will remember letting him discontent you.

learning to tap dance in adulthood

I've decided to learn to tap because it's the perfect kind of dance for my body type. I'm five-foot-ten, with a figure similar to cooked linguine.

Unfortunately, it's taken the better part of three decades to learn that tap is the dance for me. My arms are like plucked chicken wings, and in my typical dance moves, my legs resemble that trick where you make a pencil look like it's made of rubber, wiggling inexplicably.

I practice toe, heel, and I learn to shuffle. Drag one foot back and forth at a consistent beat. Like you're trying to get the gum off your sole. I've noticed little girls in line with their mothers at the grocery store doing this to keep themselves occupied. A shuffle is one of the fundamentals of tap. But if you do it too long, you look like an idiot. Or like a little girl at the store with her mother.

You should only shuffle one foot for a few beats before you switch feet or mix in another move. I don't know any other moves yet. And, as usual, I'm not sure what to do with my arms or my hands, or really the whole upper half of my body. When I practice in front of the mirror, I try not to look at anything but my feet. The sight of my arms is unsettling. I'm reminded of the Jell-O scene in *Jurassic Park*.

Tall girls learn to slouch. You can detect a girl recovering from a middle school growth spurt by the slope in her neck. She may have learned to lift her shoulders, push them back when in public, but it's hard to relearn where to set your head. Mine cocks forward, like my face is trying to escape the room.

My first long-term relationship was with a guy six inches shorter than me. I remember walking across a field hand-in-hand during a music festival and seeing the afternoon shadow of us. I looked like a mother yanking along her child.

When I brought him home, my housemate asked me if he was my little brother. I didn't own any high heels during those years. I didn't wear high heels till I was twenty-two, which is certainly no tragedy. But the ironic part is that high heels are a key tool for tall girls to unlearn their slouch. The lift of the calves forces you to finally roll your shoulders back in order to maintain balance. You have to take big leaps to catch up sometimes, which is why I'm learning to tap dance.

My nicknames have included Giraffe, String Bean, and Shaquilla (the female form of Shaq).

Next is the ball-change. I vaguely remember my childhood neighbor showing me how to step-shuffle-ball-change when I was in elementary school. I already know how to step. I think. So the ball-change will complete my ability to sequence the three together.

Tap dancers do a lot of flailing, which comes naturally to me. They also set their feet at odd angles, bend their knees slightly. I like to use these tactics while simply standing. It gets me closer to the ground.

There was a party I once attended with glow paint and people dressed as cavemen. I forget the theme. The crowd parted into a circle and chanted my name as I danced—chicken wings flapping, pencil legs wiggling, just like in a movie. I wish I could have looked down on myself and taken notes on those moves. I wished I'd been sober enough to remember what I did to earn the chanting. Two-syllable names are made to be chanted, and luckily, someone in that crowd knew my name. I'm sure the reason they chanted was because my dancing was so absurd. And shameless. I want to feel that way again, shamelessly absurd.

During that time, my best friend was barely five-feet tall. She sometimes called me "G" for Giraffe. I envied how she could blend in when she wanted. One year she had a drag queen–themed birthday party. I wore a bubblegum-colored wig and a metallic dress. On my way to the bathroom, a guy stopped me in the hallway.

He sucked off his joint and blew smoke in my face, then said, "Wait...so are you, like, actually a dude? Or no?"

In the living room, I lined up behind several other girls, waiting my turn to take a lap on the catwalk. Someone had built it from plywood as a party centerpiece. I strutted down the plank, shaking my hips. No one chanted my name. My shame was too close to the surface. And I probably wasn't drunk enough.

I noticed in a clip of *Singing in The Rain* that Gene Kelly's arms look gelatinous like mine. But he has his prop umbrella to hang onto, lampposts to swing around, pockets to hide his hands in. I think of what sort of props I could use to hide my hands. Perhaps the usual: a book, a phone, my pockets. I've given up smoking. Maybe some millennial tap dancers have already made up a dance where they text while they tap. If all else fails, I will practice my jazz hands. I will try to swing my arms at a steady rate like Gene.

It's not sensual, it's not sexy, but it is a dance that I can do where it looks the way it's supposed to. I couldn't say the same about that time I took a Zumba class.

I'm not complaining. I'm coming from a place of inclusive self-hate. And I'm seeking a place of inclusive self-love. From the outside, it appears that self-love is a community. (I imagine it's filled with the women who wear Birkenstocks and men who buy dried beans in bulk. I study them at the health food store to discover their secrets.) If this—learning to tap—is self-love, it's actually quite lonely. But it's loneliness in the best way possible. It's the kind of lonely where you feel suddenly brave enough to speak to any stranger around you. Especially if that stranger is wearing spandex and sparkly knee socks. Especially if she is a half-beat behind.

non-refundable

At the Doubletree Hotel, the leader of the movement told us how she rid herself of a basketball-sized tumor in less than two months without drugs or surgery. The cancer had come at what was otherwise an idyllic time in her life. Rita had a happy marriage and a home on the beach in Malibu. The conference room was filled with nearly a hundred people, but you couldn't hear a murmur of doubt, a shifting of feet, or a search for a cell phone. We already knew the story of how she'd gone from cancer-ridden to the radiant, healthy woman in front of us. It was a method of therapy that she invented. She never called it "therapy," though, perhaps for legal reasons. Mostly she referred to it as "healing work" or "processing." But we were still in awe. Her flowing white outfit, suggesting the purity of a guru, and matching white-blonde hair, emphasized her ocean-blue eyes. Even her manner of speech evoked a feeling of mysticism. The way she said the word "tumor" as *teyumor*, like she'd slain the mass with her enunciation.

Rita wasn't physically in the conference room. She was speaking to us on a video that was projected above the stage. The weekend training leader, Bob, showed the footage at the beginning of each healing workshop. Rita was the face of the organization, so she called the shots. Onstage after the video, Bob held up a large piece of glass, cut to look like a giant diamond, to represent our true selves. He told us that this afternoon we were going to remove all of the dirt and minerals that were caked over our diamonds.

Rita had spoken in the video about how uncovering traumatic memories could heal the body. This was done through a specific step-by-step process of visualizations and prompting questions, which would spontaneously uncover cell memories, allowing them to regenerate in a normal, healthy fashion. I sought relief from the debilitating stomachaches I'd experienced on an almost daily basis since middle school. I also hoped to be freed from my incredibly low self-esteem. I had wanted to go to counseling since I was fourteen, but my parents weren't the therapy types. And I didn't want them to think they had done something wrong to have raised a daughter who asked for psychotherapy as a birthday gift.

So I used the usual therapy replacements that could be obtained by a teenager.

At twenty, I was the youngest person attending the seminar by at least a decade, maybe two. I wasn't surprised that the group was made up of what looked like mostly upper-middle class retirees. Who else had the time or money to attend the weekend-long workshop at five hundred dollars a day? The summer beforehand, when I was living and working at a yoga retreat, a co-worker told me how this program had changed her life. Her stories of transformation convinced me. So when I received a mysterious five hundred dollar direct deposit payment from the university just before the workshop payment was due, I took it as a sign that I was meant to go.

The year before, when I was a freshman, I was hired as a data collector by the university's School of Public Health for research on flu prevention. Study participants were recruited outside of the dorm cafeteria. Those who signed up were paid to either wear a face mask for a prescribed amount of time each day, use hand sanitizer regularly, or (for the lucky control group) carry on their college lives as usual. As data collector, I was paid twelve dollars an hour to sit in various high-traffic areas in the dorm and record the people I observed. Each person was represented by a tally mark in one of the three categories: wearing a facemask, using hand sanitizer, or neither.

When I told my dad about my new gig, he said it was the best job I'd ever have. I laughed at him then, but now, I think he was right.

It was the perfect job for me during my first year of college because I was being paid for my primary pastime: people-watching. And without supervision, I could do it while in a daze, with a constant loop of Spoon and CocoRosie pumping through my headphones. I watched intently, pen ready to tally in that first column, but I never saw a soul wearing a facemask. I asked my co-workers if they'd seen a mask in the wild. Nope. None had.

That was easy money. Much easier than the minimum-wage food service jobs I had worked in high school. And the mysterious deposit, a year after my job was terminated along with the study, was even easier than tallying passersby.

Bob reminded me of my elementary school principal as he spoke, narrow-eyed with a soft smile, about Rita's transformative work. Bob was completely devoted to Rita and her wisdom. I wondered what Rita had done before she'd discovered this healing method to have earned enough money for that house in Malibu. And I wondered how much wealth she had now. I looked around the room and tried to compute how much money she would make from the emotionally desperate people here. Though I was one of them, I started to pity the other workshop participants. They hung on her every word. They were intent on getting their money's worth. A physical and emotional transformation, like Rita's, for less than a couple grand? That was a steal.

The crowd erupted in applause, and Bob left the stage. I realized the morning portion of the day's training was over. I turned to the woman next to me, a spunky insurance agent named Lois who was a friend of a friend of a friend and had given me a ride from Ann Arbor to the hotel for the day.

"Are they serving us lunch?" I asked.

"I don't think so, hun," she said, grin on her face from all the inspiration. "There's a Red Lobster across the street, though." My expression must have looked helpless. She continued, "I can drive you over, if you'd like. I think a bunch of us are going."

"Oh, no thanks," I replied, certain I was without the funds to afford any sort of sea-dwelling protein. Instead, I waited in the lobby during the break and ate a series of complementary cookies from the reception desk. I had noticed a Wendy's down the interstate on the drive into town, but I didn't think I'd have time to walk there and back before the next session began.

For the first afternoon session, we were placed into groups to walk through an abbreviated version of the process. Sitting in small circular clusters of folding chairs scattered across the carpeted room, we talked through the healing stages, eyes opened, as a sort of practice for the real thing to come. I learned that Lois had struggled with an addiction to painkillers. Several of the women detailed life-shattering divorces. When it was my turn, I felt awkward talking about my problems, which must have seemed infantile to those who sat in the circle, staring at me encouragingly. Most of them had experienced more than twice the life I had and so must have collected twice the cell memories to uncover, twice the diamond-grime to remove.

After a short break, we entered the final session. This was game time. I was anxious, anticipating what deeply buried internal darkness might surface. I still had hope that this experience would change me.

First, I would lead a process. I was relieved to be paired with a young nurse, Sarah, who I'd met earlier. I felt comfortable with her. I didn't think her cell memories held anything I couldn't handle. It turned out I was right. The memory she described, and was prompted to release, seemed far from traumatic. She recounted being on a beach at night, and I braced myself for what she was about to reveal. Sexual assault? Near drowning experience? She described a group of boys who played a prank on her, jumping out of the woods, yelling, and scaring her. No physical contact, no brush with death. Luckily, her eyes were closed, so she couldn't detect any judgment that might have been apparent on my face.

When it was my turn, I was paired with Lucille, a former therapist in her seventies. I closed my eyes, seated beside her. I worried my trauma wasn't big enough. I worried that once my cells had let go and regenerated, I wouldn't be different enough to love. I heard the murmur of processing among dozens of pairs in the large room. A pulse of whimpering and sobs radiated throughout. Her voice was gentle as she guided me through visualizations into my body. I was led to my stomach and then to a memory buried within the sticky organ. It was uncomfortable, and it felt somewhat forced, yet I was still moved to tears. By the time it was over, and I had opened my eyes, I wanted to run out of the room. But when I recognized that everyone was in their own personal turmoil of memories, my panic shrank. Lucille was sweet. She introduced me to her husband, who was also a therapist, and she wrote down their phone number in my notebook. She said they'd like to have me over for dinner sometime.

Then, we were herded out of the room. Many participants disappeared to their hotel rooms to retrieve some solitude. I went to the bathroom and rested in a stall. When I returned, the chairs were rearranged into rows facing the stage once again. I took a seat close to the exit, as we waited for Bob to play Rita's final remarks of the day. Most of the attendees had signed up for the full weekend. They had been here since Thursday night and would continue training tomorrow. I was only attending the Saturday training and would leave after the evening's close.

I thought about the cost again. So, this was what I chose to do with my five hundred dollars. I looked around the room for some sign of additional perks. Didn't we get books? A pamphlet? Some handouts? The day had consisted of a morning talk, very similar to the video I had seen on the program's website before I signed up, and the chance to talk through my darkest personal moments with a stranger, who had also paid to be here. I felt ripped off. I asked the red-eyed women around me about the cost, trying to suggest it was overpriced in the most respectful manner possible, knowing that everyone's wounds were still fresh. I got answers like "This method is priceless" and "I heard there was one young artist who couldn't afford the sessions and Rita traded some paintings for training with him!"

I kept thinking about Rita's Malibu house. My resentment grew as I listened to her closing speech. She took a long, silent look around the room. Rita gave us all what felt like a moment of eye contact, even though it was a previously recorded video of her looking into a crowd five times the size in New York. The con artist, I thought.

In my mind, I began a list of all of the things I could have done with those five hundred dollars. At the time, my job was inspecting and cleaning housing co-ops for college students, but I wasn't being given enough hours. I had just interviewed at a Ben

& Jerry's, and I couldn't understand, with my previous ice cream parlor experience, why they hadn't called me back. I suspected that it had to do with my reluctance when the manager asked me if I would be comfortable pushing customers to order larger sizes. Rita would have made a great Ben & Jerry's employee. That sort of thing probably came natural to her. Salespeople were born that way.

As we exited the conference room, I looked at all the people, with their exuberant faces, their cells reborn, their diamonds scrubbed clean. We passed the Doubletree reception desk, and I grabbed a handful of cookies before walking out the door.

panty display

According to a 1976 study, when packed in large crowds, men tend to get aggressive while women tend to get nervous. Hence the all-male mosh pits at concerts and women hugging their purses in amusement parks. Typically, when I'm in crowded public places, I will do just about anything to avoid brushing up against a stranger. When I feel breath on my scalp from the guy who's standing far too close in line behind me, I balloon with rage. I already feel panic in crowded spaces. And when I cannot keep my bubble from being invaded, I want to scream. But I didn't notice how exposed I was in this moment.

Eighteen and freshly dumped, I was at the mall to forget about the loss. My friend searched the Victoria's Secret clearance bin while I sat on a meticulously layered display of thongs in the entryway, oblivious to the procession of high school girls I obstructed as I wept. The mannequins and I looked like a before-and-after tableau. *See what you'd look like without the help of a lace-lined, generously padded push-up bra? Pathetic and rejected. See what you'd look like with a beautifully coordinated teddy and stocking set? Confident and desired.*

"Are you okay?"

I looked up to see a woman with an infant strapped to her back. I noticed two more children, attached to her waist with colorful leashes. The children wriggled and twisted and pulled on their leashes, but the woman stood and looked at me with concern. I wiped my face with my jacket sleeve.

"Come here," she said.

I stood up. She hugged me. I leaned into her shoulder as she recited a prayer in my ear. Her children orbited around us, and my breathing slowed. Then she was pulled away, like a dog walker on roller skates.

Tonight, I listened to the albums I played on repeat during the months I spent recovering from that break-up. I wanted to know if the songs would still have the power they had over me almost a decade ago. I sang along while doing dishes from the dinner I'd shared with my husband. I noticed the percussive beat over the pseudo-orchestral electronic hum. I remembered my grief. I noticed the simplicity of the melody. I remembered the small kindnesses that sometimes invaded that grief. I noticed that each chorus, a looping mantra I've repeated hundreds of times, evoked an obvious cliché. I hadn't noticed that before.

bad thief

I noticed him when he crossed the street ahead of me. Once he reached my side of the road, he turned around, waited for me to pass, then followed close behind. At the end of the block was the library. I'd have to stop there to drop my videos into the return slot. I could feel him lurking a foot away. At the end of the block, I'd be waiting prey. When I reached the corner, I turned with my back against the wall as I opened my backpack. I'd heard that you should look a criminal in the face. He was pale, with close-cropped hair. He wore a puffy jacket and low-slung jeans. He looked like a Nazi. Or maybe Eminem. He reached toward me and I froze. He pulled the videos from my hands. I surprised myself and pulled them back. I was so shocked I couldn't speak. Exactly what I had feared had come to be, and it so rarely works that way. He turned and continued towards the bus stop. I remained standing there and exclaimed profanities once I regained the ability to speak.

I became afraid of running into him again. I worried he may have been humiliated by the half-assed attempt at robbery and would make up for it the next time he saw me. I was wearing a conspicuous bright red ski jacket. When I got home, I found a plain gray one and began wearing only that one from then on.

Days later, I did see him again. It was the second time my paranoia foretold reality. He walked into a coffee shop with a girl who must have been my age and probably went to college too. I couldn't believe he was a person who went to coffee shops with cute girls. I nearly laughed at myself for being so scared of him. Bad guys didn't drink lattes.

bad mentor

I used to want to be an artist.

In college, I took painting classes during the summer, went to drop-in life-drawing sessions, and did a few commissioned paintings and murals.

In late August before my senior year, I received a mass e-mail announcing that there would be an artist in residence during the fall semester. He was looking for student interns to help him with a near-life-sized board game. In exchange for their help, he would provide mentorship to students. He was famous for elaborate art installations and realistic comics rife with social commentary. He worked in artistic realms I was unfamiliar with. I was fascinated.

I met him at Starbucks a few days after replying to the e-mail. I had looked him up online, so he was easy to spot. He was the short, bald guy in the worn jean jacket, looking around just beyond the vestibule. I introduced myself.

"I see there's a Buffalo Wild Wings across the street. Do you want to get a real drink?" He said he had just gotten into town from across the country the day before.

He sat at the bar. I took the vacant stool beside him. It was noon, but you wouldn't know if it was day or night in the darkened side of the restaurant we occupied. He ordered a Jack Daniels. Liquor consumption set off an alarm in my young female brain. *Was he going to hit on me?* I debated whether to order a lemonade or alcohol. I didn't want to be rude. I also didn't want to look like a pussy.

"You're getting a drink, right?" He acknowledged me for the first time since we sat down. "It's on me."

Despite being a college student, I wasn't a day drinker. I also had shit tolerance. I'd never been to a meeting that involved alcohol, and I didn't want to start rambling or ranting the way I did when I got tipsy. I didn't know if I would be selected to intern with him. But I had a hunch that not drinking would hurt my interview (or whatever this was) more than slurring a few words would. He'd already made quick work of his whiskey and ordered another. I ordered a hard cider.

"Attagirl!"

I asked him about the project, but he responded with the same one-line description of the installation from the e-mail I'd already read. Before I could question further, his mind somehow jumped to another artist, a colleague of his out west who'd been commissioned a half-million dollar sculpture of a famous athlete. He said they'd gone out to dinner recently and the asshole wouldn't pick up the bill.

He told me that all artists were like that—cocky, self-absorbed, and competitive. He said the worst part about teaching art was being in competition with your own students. He said teachers like the sculptor would go so far as to sabotage their own students.

I thought about the information I'd gathered about this man on his website. He'd been championed as a voice of the people. His art was lauded for its push for social justice and representations of the working class.

He mentioned his ex-wife, trailing off before any meaning could be transmitted. I only gathered the fact that he had an ex-wife, which was maybe all he had wanted to get across. He drained his drink and ordered another. His gaze drifted to the television. Upon delivery of his new whisky, he slammed his empty glass on the bar and began yelling at the newscaster. Then he stood up and swiveled around, his chest jutting out.

"Huh! Hey!" He pecked his head forward. He was looking for someone to fight. No one took him up on it. Most of the people here were on their lunch breaks.

I finished half of my drink when he finished his third. We left the bar and he asked for directions to the bus stop. Then he gave me his cell number. He said the university was putting him up in a depressing apartment. He walked towards the landmark I described, a statue of a naked couple holding up a naked child, and it dawned on me that I had the intern position.

At the first organized meeting for the installation, a dozen students gathered in the gallery space. I overheard that most were in the art program and were required to participate for course credit. The artist read work roles off of a hotel notepad and asked students to raise their hands when they heard one that appealed to them. I chose graphic imaging because I wanted to learn something new. Once the students gathered into their work groups, our cluster of four computer nerds huddled around the only table and chair in the gallery, where he sat, slouching back and ready to give orders. He hadn't stood once during the meeting. The other students were visibly nervous. Not everyone had gotten the happy hour interview. He pulled a flask out of his jean jacket pocket and took a swig, then set it on the table alongside his pad of paper and sketches. We made eye contact and I raised my eyebrows and nodded to the flask, out in the open, in a school—a post-secondary art school, but a school, nonetheless.

"So what?" he shrugged. He smirked. He got pleasure out of pushing the boundaries. And I think he was pleased I had pointed it out. I wondered what had happened in his adolescence that left him stuck there. Massive social rejection, maybe. Was this why he seemed so occupied with impressing college students? Or maybe he was just trying to get laid. This was a guy, I admit, I probably would have been impressed by if I'd met him as a freshman. But by twenty-one, I felt I was grown. He was older. He was an artist. But he wasn't innovative; he was nowhere near original.

goodbye yellow brick road

He is charismatic and pushy. I admire this because I am passive and insecure. I met Elton in the tenth grade at the afternoon arts center where I took classes to escape kids at my regular high school. When you get a chance to redefine yourself in adolescence, you take it. And Elton was the person after whom I decided I would model my new, confident self.

Elton likes to dance in the middle of the circle of desks before class. He touches people he barely knows, cupping their faces in his hands and squealing about a new anime that is *so so amazing!* He has eyelashes that are thicker and longer than the packaged kind at the drugstore. They curl up and away from his lids, making his eyes appear even larger and wider than they already are. Some days he wears eyeliner, sparkly eye shadow, and rainbow jewelry. Other days he is plain-faced and wears all black.

We catch a ride with my brother in the Astrovan he's just purchased for two hundred dollars. The van reeks of cigarettes, and the insides are matted with dog fur. The backseat storage compartments are decorated with foam alphabet stickers. You can imagine the chain-smoking mother who used to drive the car. I picture her with bleached hair, appeasing her children with gas station stops for slurpees. This provides a stark contrast with my brother, who is frequently described as "Death Metal Jesus" due to his musical tastes and facial hair choices. My brother pops a tape into the deck and the sound of buzzing drums and throaty growls blasts our ears.

"This sounds like frogs mating," Elton says.

If I had put in the tape, I would have resentfully switched over to the radio after that comment. I am sensitive to perceived criticism and take everything personally. But my brother continues to nod his head to the sparse bass drum thumps and chuckles good-naturedly at the comment.

My brother drops us off at a musty vintage store, which is

packed floor to ceiling with 1960s polyester and cracked pleather. I follow Elton up and down the aisles agreeing with his views on leather fringe versus yarn fringe, what style of heel is most flattering. When he gets bored, we leave out the back exit. In the parking lot he opens his palm to reveal a patch the size of a playing card.

"Look what I got."

"You stole that?" I am shocked. I have never shoplifted, and I can't fathom doing it so nonchalantly. I especially can't understand taking such a risk for the reward of a crusty UAW patch. I'm angry that he put me at risk of being his accomplice. But I don't say anything.

After school one day, Elton asks if he can come over. My parents are still at work, so I say yes, and we walk the three blocks to my house. When I open the door, he struts in ahead of me and proclaims he is hungry. He goes to the kitchen like he's been in my house before and opens the fridge. As usual, there isn't anything exciting: a bag of carrots, a tub of miso, and a loaf of cardboard-like sprouted bread. He opens the freezer.

He gasps, "Let's make veggie burgers!" I understand that this means, "Make me a veggie burger."

Once we have our burgers, we take our plates to the living room. Elton spots the *Fight Club* VHS next to the TV. "Let's watch *Fight Club*!"

The way he starts each emphatic sentence with "Let's" and pairs it with some dance-y arm gesture could convince me that anything is fun. If he said, "Let's scrub the bathtub!" I'd probably be on board, a sense of thrill as I put on the rubber gloves.

I soon find out that Elton doesn't want to actually watch the whole movie. He has the remote in one hand and the sandwich in the other, and he's fast-forwarding to the part where a penis flashes on the screen for a millisecond. He's trying to get it to pause at the exact spot, but the picture is crackly when you pause it, and it takes a dozen tries. I know my dad is coming home soon, and I wonder when Elton is going to give up.

I enjoy Elton's attention at school, but I no longer seek him out. He asks me if I'm going to my school's production of *The Wizard of Oz*. He has friends in the play, so he invites me to go with him. My mom drops us off, and we find seats in the middle section. He sets his jacket down, then goes to look for other friends. He sits beside a blonde girl I don't recognize. My classmate's mom in the row in front of me turns around and asks how my family is doing. I feel pathetic sitting here alone, talking to a mom. Elton does not come back to the seat during the first act, or the second. At intermission, he finds me and says he has a ride home. I go to the bathroom. When I return to my seat, his jacket is gone. This is the last time we hang out. I feel relieved.

stranger parts

It is a stranger part of the city. At the street's dead end, there is a fire pit and a rusted-out pickup truck on one side, and a thick cluster of trees on the other. A few steps between two pines on the wooded side leads to a clearing where the trees encircle patchy grass, a decaying wooden stage with a broken piano. Inside this circle of trees you feel like you're at a music festival where everyone's left you behind. Here, you might trick yourself into thinking that the solitude of nature is boundless, until you look up to see the billboards looming. The one directly above depicts a surgically-enhanced lawyer with spotlights shining on her ten-foot-wide lips.

I hide here, escaping a party that is taking place around the fire pit. In solitude, I am gathering the mental energy to interact with strangers. Hunched-over partygoers encircle the fire: a variety of people who look like they're in a *No Exit* type of situation, like a jury call or a line at the pharmacy could only bring this array of people together. But somehow only one or two degrees separate each person.

I finally muster the confidence to rejoin the group, so I leave the circle of trees to find Taylor, who's brought me here. Taylor thinks people with facial piercings or extremist ideologies are automatically fascinating. All of the people here fascinate her. While she talks with nearly every guest, I observe. I notice a guy with a hood shadowing his face. He stumbles around, mumbling at the women next to him. I watch him stumble his way beside the pickup, lean forward with his hands clutching his prick, and urinate on the rusted wheel. After he pulls up his zipper, he comes back to the circle of people and teeters over the fire. He groans and then falls into the flames.

After a couple guys pull him out of the fire pit, Taylor tells me to come with her to the house next door. Inside, she sits on the floor among several others: a girl with feathers attached to her hair, a guy with black lipstick, and a few who are more nondescript and therefore less fascinating. A guy pulls out several jars of weed and offers samples. I hope it won't make me feel paranoid because then I'll have even less fun. But I also hope not to get so relaxed I fall into the fire.

Later, as we pull away from the dead end, Taylor's car is waved down by a friend of a friend. Jerry has a wild mass of hair that stands up into rays, which make his head look like a cartoon sun. He wears suspenders hanging at the sides of his wide black pants. Taylor agrees to give him a ride, and he slides into the back seat beside me. In the front, Taylor is seated next to one of the guys from inside the house. Jerry and I somehow discover we went to the same high school. He tells me he was expelled in the eleventh grade, so he just dropped out. I asked him why he was expelled. He said he brought a machete to school, but he had found it on the sidewalk that morning, so it was just a misunderstanding. Then he bragged that he used to sell acid-soaked sticks of gum to the freshmen in the parking lot. I scooch over, closer to the fogging window, and he notices.

He turns and says, "Do you like fun?" I turn to him and cannot think of a response.

"I think you've got some issues, girl."

"Yeah, okay," I answer.

"You've got some sand in your vagina, that's for sure."

I think that if this were true, I'd be at home watching TV right now.

He turns his attention to Taylor and Dan up front. I meditate on the concept of sand in places it shouldn't be. I wonder if he tripped on the machete when he found it, lying on the ground.

We drop off Jerry. Dan goes home with Taylor. I return to my rightful place: the living room couch in my parents' house, where I can still catch the tail end of *Saturday Night Live*.

my hangover cure is your hangover

At the concert I felt out of place, so I stood at the periphery and watched the audience. A girl with long red hair and glasses held herself up by clutching the sleeves of a young man, a boy really. She swayed to the electronic beat, the operatic voices. Her eyes appeared to be filled with tears, but it could have been the glare of spotlights against her glasses. Though the boy had clearly brought her here, their mental paths must have parted somewhere along the bar. He might have been her boyfriend. She might have only thought that he was her boyfriend. The musicians onstage, sisters wearing painted mustaches, began my favorite song. I turned to the girl beside me. She was still attached to the boy and yelling, "Yesss!" Her head lurched forward. The boy took a step toward the stage. The girl's body buckled. She pulled herself up by his forearm. He bobbed his head as if there weren't a human-sized barnacle seizing beside him. She sang along: "I just want to be your housewife." She grabbed both of his biceps and tried turning him towards her—"I'll iron your clothes"—but he kept looking at the stage. I wanted him to love her because she felt so strongly that she needed it. She continued singing: "I'll make your bed." She ignored the musicians' sad sarcasm and swapped it for sing-song shouting. She was looking up to where she thought his eyes were gazing at her own. But she couldn't make out his line of vision because of her tears. Or her glasses-glare. I imagined the next morning she might wake up alone in her own bed, and, later, beside a mug filled with coffee, or smoothie, or raw eggs, compose an e-mail to her best friend about her boyfriend and their unforgettable night together.

acknowledgements

Several of these pieces previously appeared in online publications, some with slightly different titles. *Cheap Pop* published "Six Years Ago" and "My Hangover Cure is Your Hangover," and *The Billfold* published "Non-Refundable."

Big thanks to everyone at Etchings Press who helped turn this collection of essays into my first book. Thank you to my friends, family, teachers, and students. In particular, I'd like to thank my parents (Kathy and Edwin), in-laws (Pattie and Chuck), Eddie, Sam, Gayle, Mandy, Felicia, Caitlin, Mary, and anyone who thinks writing isn't stupid. The biggest thank you goes to Josh, who convinced me that my writing isn't stupid.

colophon

The cover text and titles are set in American Typewriter.
The body text is in Angleterre Book.

author biography

Shannon McLeod teaches high school English in Southeast Michigan. Her writing has previously appeared in *Hobart*, *Gawker*, *The Billfold*, *Cheap Pop*, and *Word Riot*, among other publications. You can find her on www.shannon-mcleod.com.

etchings press

Etchings Press is a student-run publisher at the University of Indianapolis. Each year, student editors choose the Whirling Prize, a post-publication award, in the fall and coordinate a publication contest for one poetry chapbook, one prose chapbook, and one novella in the spring. For more information, please visit etchings.uindy.edu.

Previous winners and publications

Poetry
2019: *As Lovers Always Do* by Marne Wilson
2018: *In the Herald of Improbable Misfortunes* by Robert Campbell
2017: *Uncle Harold's Maxwell House Haggadah* by Danny Caine
2016: *Some Animals* by Kelli Allen
2015: *Velocity of Slugs* by Joey Connelly
2014: *Action at a Distance* by Christopher Petruccelli

Prose
2019: *Dissenting Opinion from the Committee for the Beatitudes* by Marc J. Sheehan (fiction)
2018: *The Forsaken* by Chad V. Broughman (fiction)
2017: *Unravelings* by Sarah Cheshire (memoir)
2016: *Pathetic* by Shannon McLeod (essays)
2015: *Ologies* by Chelsea Biondolillo (essays)
2014: *Static: Stories* by Frederick Pelzer (fiction)

Novella
2019: *Savonne, Not Vonny* by Robin Lee Lovelace
2018: *Edge of the Known Bus Line* by James R. Gapinski
2017: *The Denialist's Almanac of American Plague and Pestilence* by Christopher Mohar
2016: *Followers* by Adam Fleming Petty

www.ingramcontent.com/pod-product-compliance
Lightning Source LLC
Chambersburg PA
CBHW060034040426
42333CB00042B/2445

www.ingramcontent.com/pod-product-compliance
Lightning Source LLC
Chambersburg PA
CBHW070035040426
4233CB000040B/1680

AFTERWORD

I hope this book was able to help you to understand the basics of negotiation – including strategies, methods and techniques essential in your daily life.

The next step is to apply each strategy at home, school and work. Also reflect and consider the importance of negotiation and communication in nurturing positive relationships with others – be it your family, friends or work colleagues.

until the other person is ready or capable of hearing what you have to say.

The mere act of acknowledging barriers to communications can give you the opportunity to work together to start to agree on how to resolve the barriers. Then it will be easier to discuss and resolve the real issues.

settlement conference put aside you personal issues and clear your mind. If the other issues are such that you can't do this, don't start the negotiation. Ask for a postponement or send someone else. You need to have all of you faculties focused to do the job properly. Such distractions are barriers or obstacles that stand in the way of a successful negotiation. Better put, barriers are obstacles to effective communications.

In order to have an effective discussion, the parties to the discussion have to be able to hear, be heard, and understand each other. If you sense the other person is distracted, make it your responsibility to expose the cause. If it is going to impede the other person from listening or focusing on what you are saying, you may want to suggest postponing the meeting. If you feel it will cause the other person to rush through the meeting and grant concessions to wrap things up, then it may be advantageous to proceed. Until you know the situation, you can't judge what the impact will be on the negotiations.

You may actually want to call their attention to the fact that they weren't listening and ask them why. While this second tactic may seem rude, it can often uncover the reason for the barrier that can then be removed. For example, I recall a situation where the other person replied, "I'm really sorry, my daughter is very sick and I'm distracted." To this I said that I was sorry to hear about her daughter and we put off further discussions until the personal problem was resolved. In understanding her personal need, we dealt with each other as real people. This helped us to overcome some of the tougher issues we were facing as we had built up a level of trust and respect. The point is that unless communications are being heard, they should be forestalled

in a hurry because they think that you're not pressured on closing the deal. So what do these negotiators do? They offer countless negotiations as their way of giving you the option of saying YES.

- DON'T TAKE the negotiation issues personally. Negotiations tend to fail because one or both parties get easily affected by personal issues that aren't related to the entire deal. Always remember that you won't become a successful negotiator if you're making a fuss out of other's personal lives instead of looking for solutions in closing the deal. If the other party is rude or hard to deal with, understand their behavior and focus on the objective side of the negotiation.

- EXPECT the best outcome in negotiating. Successful negotiators are perceived by many as positive-thinkers. If they expect more, they'll give more. One proven tactic in achieving positive negotiation results is by opening an extreme position for others to agree/disagree. Optimism is a self-fulfilling insight. If you're positive about the outcome of your negotiation, then you'll end up with less-satisfying outcome – no conflicts and personal attacks between agreed deals.

Negotiators are human. They are subject to being distracted by personal problems, other matters and even exhaustion. To a lesser extent, they can be distracted by delays in a meeting, antagonistic behaviour of someone in the room, or even by the light coming in through the window.

Being comfortable is an essential ingredient to being effective as a negotiator or mediator. Before entering a

sions only to get something from the person. When you give anything without letting other parties reciprocate, they'll become entitled to your concessions.

- SHOW THE PERSON you're negotiating with how his needs should be met. A successful negotiator is always looking for situation coming from perspectives of the other side. Everyone has a different view of the world, so you might be way ahead of the negotiating game if you figured out other's perception of the deal. Instead of trying to win the entire negotiation, seek ways that will make the other negotiator/s feel contented.

- FOCUS ON DEALING with the pressure from the other side instead of yours. Sometimes, we have the tendency to look at our own pressure, which is one of the reasons why we are making a deal with others. When we focus on our own limitations, we're missing the big picture. Some negotiators often ask this question: "What do you know about the pressure coming from the other side?" Your answer likely reflects your capacity in recognizing the reasons from the other side. If you discovered that they're under pressure, try looking for ways to utilize that pressure in order to achieve better results within yourself.

- DON'T HURRY TOO MUCH. Patience matters in a successful negotiation. A lot of negotiators can attest to this: When a person rushes while negotiating with another person, they're more likely to commit mistakes. Patience can be quite devastating for some negotiators, especially if they're

12

TIPS FOR SUCCESSFUL NEGOTIATION

One's ability to negotiate in today's business environment can easily determine the difference between failure and success. In line with this, below are seven tips on how to become successful in negotiating with anyone.

- Do not be afraid in asking for what you want. Most successful negotiators are assertive and love taking challenges. That being said, they almost know everything that is negotiable (negotiation consciousness). Being assertive in your negotiations means asking for what you want and saying NO for the right reasons. Take note that there is a big difference between being assertive and aggressive.

- Do NOT GIVE anything without receiving something in return. Unilateral concessions are deemed "self-defeating". In other words, whenever you give something, you'll also get something in return ("I'll give you this if you'll give me that"). When negotiating, don't ask for additional conces-

situation wherein individuals can benefit from taking into action the ways of resolving issues.

According to researchers Russell Spears, Tom Postmes and Marijn Van Zomeren, collective action involves the use of identity, efficacy and injustice in closing the gap between parties. The researchers recently conducted a survey to target over 190 in-depth studies on the socio-psychological impact of collective action.

by the Nobel Prize on Economic Sciences for their outstanding contributions in game theory.

DISPUTE RESOLUTION

Dispute resolution is the process of resolving conflicts or disputes between two or more parties involved. Methods in dispute resolution include facilitation, conciliation, mediation, collaborative law and litigation (lawsuits).

In this process, a party can theoretically use verbal attacks or violence. However, most dispute resolution experts do not recommend this. Some people believe that violent acts can put an end to conflicts. In some cases however, it often escalates them.

Dispute resolution has two major types:

- Consensual Process – This is where conciliation, collaborative law and litigation fall. Here, parties are given time to explain their agreement.

- Adjudicative Process – This involves arbitration in which the judge, jury or arbitrators identifies the outcome.

Dispute resolution is required in taking legal actions, mediation and negotiations at court, and government offices. However, not all disputes are being resolved regardless of the gravity of the case within the parties.

COLLECTIVE ACTION

Collective action is defined as any action aimed to let two or more negotiating parties use their representative to speak up on resolving any issue or conflict. This action is widely used in economics, political science, sociology and psychology. Collective action problem refers to a particular

46   PATRICK KENNEDY

third-party assistance in resolving negotiation issues. When
the conflict is severe and the disputants are having a hard
time talking to each other peacefully, mediators can set
them into separate contact then help them in working on a
settlement or "cease-fire". Arbitration meanwhile is done by
allowing the third-party to listen and speak up on both sides
before rendering a decision.

GAME THEORY

Game theory is an in-depth study of tactical decision-
making between two or more parties. In formal terms, it is
defined as "the study of arithmetical models of cooperation
and conflict between rational, intelligent decision-makers".

Game theory is generally used in psychology, political
science and economics, as well as biology and philosophy.
This theory applies to an extensive range of human behavioral relations, and has consistently developed into an
"umbrella term" referring to logistical aspects of decision-
making between parties.

Game theory began to modernize after John Von
Neumann developed the Two-Person, Zero-Sum, a "fixed-
point" theoretical approach in allowing solutions to close
the gap between two or more parties involved in a particular
situation. The development of the Two-Person, Zero-Sum
was followed by the release of Von Neumann's book, Theory
of Games and Economic Behavior in 1944.

Game theory was developed in the early 1950s by many
academic scholars. It was later applied in Biology by the
1970s. Since then, it has been recognized as one of the most
significant tools in closing the gap between parties negotiating. In 2011, eight American game theorists were recognized

11

CLOSING THE GAP BETWEEN PARTIES

I n this chapter, we'll discuss four basic ways on how to close the gap between parties when negotiating. These are conflict resolution, game theory, dispute resolution and collective action.

CONFLICT RESOLUTION

Conflict resolution is any form of reduction from severity of a conflict between two or more parties. It also refers to conflict management in which the parties involved adjust to less extreme tactics by means of settlement.

THIRD-PARTY INVOLVEMENT in Conflict Resolution

Third parties usually become more involved in conflict resolution. They are either being called by the first two parties as "disputants" or acting up on their own perspectives because the conflict aggravates them.

Mediation and arbitration are two forms of the so-called third-party intervention. Mediation involves the role of

- Build rewarding, strong and trusting relationships, resolve conflicts, solve problems and think creatively.

- Stay motivated to empathize or understand the person you're talking to, even if there are times you're not comfortable with what he/she is saying.

- Fully understand yourself including situations that are causing you trouble and/or what you really want in life.

- Empathize or understand situations troubling others.

10

EMOTIONAL AWARENESS

Emotions play a crucial role in how we communicate at home, school or work. It refers to the way we feel and think that motivates us to make decisions or communicate. The way you react to non-verbal cues or signs affects your understanding towards other people and how they understand you in return.

If you aren't in touch with your emotions, then you won't understand how others feel or why you're feeling that way (which often results to having a difficult time communicating with your needs or feelings).

Emotional awareness has a way to provide you tools necessary for understanding yourself and other people. Although recognizing your feelings may seem too simple, a lot of people tend to ignore or try sedating stronger emotions like fear, sadness and anger. That being said, your ability to communicate depends on how you connect yourself to your emotions. This is referred to as emotional awareness. It has the ability to manage all your emotions in the pursuit of effective communication, and helps you:

create a good investment in your communication and even relationship.

- Put in humor between conversations. If it's used in the right time, humor is an awesome way to manage stress while communicating. When things are becoming too serious for both of you, crack up a joke or share an entertaining story.

Power Negotiation - Getting To The YES

their body language and figure out its effective side. Notice how people react to each other when something happens. Also try figuring out the relationship between these people, what they're exactly talking about, and how each feels towards the situation.

STRESS MANAGEMENT

Even in the smallest scenarios, stress triggers you to do tasks under pressure. However, when stress becomes too overwhelming or constant, it can hinder one's communication by disrupting his/her capacity to come up with creative ideas or think clearly. When you're stressed, there are tendencies that you'll misread other people's way of saying things, send unnecessary non-verbal signs or, worse, show misbehavior.

When stress occurs, you can always manage it by taking a break from work, meditating, enrolling in yoga sessions or taking a walk at the park with a friend or significant other. Doing these activities will help reduce stress within hours. In addition, when you have a relaxed, stress-free mindset, you'll remain emotionally engaged while communicating with anyone.

TIPS ON MANAGING **Stress while Communicating:**

- If possible, agree to disagree. In other words, take some time from the situations causing you stress and meditate. Find a place wherein you can regain your normal mindset.

- Have the willingness to compromise. If you realize that the person you're talking to cares a lot about something that you do, then compromising may be a bit easier. This will

their words into your head. Doing this will strengthen your ability in listening.

Non-verbal Communication

When we talk about things we always care about, we do this by using non-verbal signs or wordless methods like our facial expressions, body movements or posture. The way we move, listen, look and react to others simply tells them more about what you feel.

When we develop our ability to use non-verbal communication in understanding, we connect ourselves with others – express our feelings through body language, navigate daunting situations, and nurture positive relationships.

You can use "open" body language in enhancing your communication effectively. An open body language means maintaining an eye contact with the person you're talking to, sitting/standing properly, and keeping arms uncrossed.

Tips on How to Improve Non-verbal Communication:

- Try looking at non-verbal signs as a group. Do not read too much or oversee a particular non-verbal cue or gesture. If possible, consider all the non-verbal signs you receive – from body language to the tone of your voice to eye contact.

- Always consider individual differences. People from different walks of life tend to use various non-verbal communication tactics or gestures, so it's very important for you to consider the age, gender, culture, religion and emotional state of the person you're communicating with. Asians and Hispanics are likely to use non-verbal signs.

- Observe people in public areas such as parks, shopping malls, coffee shops, restaurants, or railway stations. Observe

becoming intense, listening to each other can help relieve those emotions and resolve issues as well.

- Saves time by clarifying information to avoid misunderstanding or conflict.

- Creates an environment wherein everyone has the right to express their feelings, opinions and ideas without hurting anyone's feelings or being threatened by others.

- Lets the speaker feel heard and understood. This way, both of you will build deeper, stronger relationships.

EFFECTIVE LISTENING TIPS:

- Always show interest in what is being said. Smile at the person you're communicating with, nod in between interesting conversations, and make sure that you maintain a good posture.

- Avoid looking judgmental. For a meaningful and effective communication, you don't need to like every detail that's being talked about. But that doesn't mean you're going to put a lot of criticisms or blame to it. You need to set aside your verdict by withholding criticisms or blame to understand what the person is saying.

- Avoid interruptions. Redirecting the entire conversation to your concerns (i.e. telling the person, "If you think it's not good, let me tell you what really happened in my case") is a big no! Keep in mind that listening isn't the same as waiting for your turn to blabber. Give the person the right to say what he wants to say.

- Focus on the speaker – from his body language to other non-verbal cues. Stop daydreaming and checking your messages in your phone every minute while he's talking. If you find focusing on other speakers hard to do, try repeating

by deepening your connection with people and improving your problem-solving, decision-making, and team building skills. It also enables you to use unconstructive messages without destroying trust or respect. In fact, effective communication uses a combination of skills like attentive listening and non-verbal communication, and the ability to recognize your own emotions and the people you're dealing with.

METHODS IN IMPROVING **Communication**

While we all know that communication is a skill that we learn everyday, it is actually "more effective" when it's being shown spontaneously. For example, a speech that is being read alone has quite a big impact on the speech delivered to others especially when it is spontaneous.

However, improving your communication takes time and effort. The more time and effort you spend in practicing your skills, the more spontaneous and instinctive your communication will be.

EFFECTIVE LISTENING

Listening is one of the most important aspects of successful communication. When you listen, you understand the words and other information delivered by the person. In other words, listening means understanding carefully how the speaker feels towards any stuff you're talking about.

EFFECTIVE LISTENING:

- Relieves downbeat emotions. When emotions are

9

WHY COMMUNICATION IS STILL KEY AND METHODS TO IMPROVE YOURS?

Communication helps us understand a person or situation. It enables us to solve problems, settle differences with others, create an environment wherein we can generate ideas, and build respect, trust and affection.

However, communication is also a considerable factor why conflict happens between two people. Some people make use of it to ruin one's reputation. Communication is also used in creating professional disputes. Because of this, established relationships are jeopardized.

EFFECTIVE COMMUNICATION – **What is it All About?**

In this day and age, we receive, process and send messages regularly. Nonetheless, effective communication is more than just exchanging necessary information. Effective communication is also about having a clear understanding of the emotional factors behind that information.

Effective communication develops fruitful relationships at home, school, work as well as social encounters. It is done

late outcomes with cues that they cannot relate to most of the time. For example, if a redhead bombshell wearing tight pants and stilettos ignores you, but flirts with your boyfriend, you'll become suspicious of other women who are just like the bombshell.

- You don't have any idea that everything happens in front of your eyes. Sometimes, we don't get to notice the major details in our surroundings probably because of callousness. Because of this, our perception is going out of nowhere and that affects our way of thinking or dealing with others. You also miss out on the necessary information and lose control towards normal things. Having the right perception is important because it gives you a clearer understanding about the things going on around you.

- Your first perception affects your succeeding perceptions. When you encounter negative situations or reactions to yourself, how much of that "perceptive effect" affects you? Here's an example: if your first experience in undergoing therapy was not good, think how that perception will affect your succeeding perceptions.

- Perception allows you to reconstruct memories. Your past memories are likely influenced by situations or interactions that occurred from the first event. Some people use perception as a language in influencing others to create memories. But in certain cases, one's perception or memory of what happened ten years ago might not become accurate ten years later.

- Perception allows you to let myths oversee your responses. Imagine you're in a workplace, and you see a colleague crying. If you think that the tears streaming in his eyes are a sign of weakness, then you'll have a perception that the colleague is true to his feelings and sensitive over some things.

8
—————

UNDERSTANDING HOW TO USE
PERCEPTION TO YOUR ADVANTAGE

One of the things we do when resolving a problem is changing our perception about that problem. But sometimes, people tend to resist in changing their perceptions – only to assume that they're right in what they hear, see or remember.

The truth which perhaps not everyone knows is that perceptions are accurate, most especially in situations triggered by human emotions. In this chapter, we'll discuss the importance of understanding perception in our daily experiences.

- Perception affects your capability in focusing. When you've got ideas in your head, you often search for evidences that will likely support each idea. This process is referred to as confirmation bias. If you think you're the luckiest person to wear a red T-shirt on New Year's Eve, then you're focusing on the beliefs coming from other people. Your perception is reflected by the things you're looking for evidence or paying attention to.

- Perception allows you to classify experiences (and even people) into categories. People tend to learn how to corre-

Value is considered the most essential component of negotiating since this allows you to gauge the objectives of other parties. Once a successful negotiation is achieved, both parties now have the prerogative to highlight any key details, then share it to non-involving parties without creating any conflict.

4. Vision

Vision is also as essential as value since gives both parties an option to visualize the possible outcome of what they've negotiated. Vision allows a party to understand the "quiet motivations" of what has been talked about via images presented from the other party (and vice versa).

5. Understanding Yourself

Before we begin to understand the objective side of negotiating with others, we need to understand ourselves first. This doesn't need any further explanations: It is imperative that we invest effective negotiations by assessing ourselves. The idea of "understanding" in negotiations lies beneath optimizing strengths and minimizing weaknesses.

Power Negotiation - Getting To The YES

quite easy to forget that we deal with an individual or group who has more aspirations than we do. In negotiating, always remember that the facts and figure don't only matter. It is clear that many of us are likely dealing with those we trust, rather than others we can't share our interests with.

To establish good relationships with people we are negotiating with, try focusing on certain elements given by "counter-parties". Don't forget the human elements, as well.

2. Process

This negotiating component has a lot to do with asking yourself these questions:

- Have I spent time thinking about a particular agenda for my upcoming negotiation?

- Do I have the necessary templates or tools to support the usefulness of the entire negotiation?

- Will the negotiation ensure my desired minutes of dealing with others?

- Will I take note all the concessions received or given by other parties?

Tip: Write down these questions in your journal for better assessment of your negotiation with others.

3. Value

Value is another negotiating component that has lot to do with asking questions such as:

- What are the facts and figures supporting the entire negotiating environment?

- What are the key objectives I need in pursuing an effective negotiation with other parties?

- What alternative/s does each party involved have?

7

THE INTRICACIES AND COMPONENTS
OF A NEGOTIATION

I n negotiation, two people are usually involved – one achieving his/her goals while the other walking away due to disappointment in the outcome of what has been talked about (or vice versa).

In a study conducted by The Negotiation Academy, 35% of the 430 businesses they targeted spend 1/3 of their 24/7 activity in negotiating. That being said, businesses are more into this move, instead of individuals. In fact, the word "negotiation" has become synonymous in business deals or transactions.

COMPONENTS OF A NEGOTIATION

Explained below are the five components of negotiating that not only businesses, but also individuals should consider.

1. Relationship

Don't forget that all of us negotiate with others. It is

Power Negotiation - Getting To The YES　31

Strategy #29: **Do not Yield** – again according to Billikopf, it might seem noble to yield on vital issues, but it destroys a relationship. He advices that you should not ask the other party to consider your opinion, but rather look for compromises, such as stretching.

. . .

STRATEGY #23: **Sit Down** - This indicates to the other individual to the negotiation that some considerable amount time will be consumed to listen to their side or bargain. Never ask the other individual to speak if you are not going to spare sufficient time to listen.

Strategy #24: Lean in - moving in towards the conversation shows interest. In addition, head nods help in making the other party know that their concepts are being followed. However, constant nodding or repeatedly saying "right" will appear hypocritical.

Strategy #25: Keep Your Cool – generally all experts agree on these ground rules for problems in communication. There should be no walking away or yelling.

Strategy #26: Be Precise – according to Billikopf, you should always be direct to the point. In addition, the parties ought to keep off words like "we disagree," or phrases that put a person to a defensive position.

Strategy #27: Avoid Empty Threats – although instilling fear can be powerful, it is advisable that you use it sparingly. Issuing empty threats will reduce the other individual's respect for you.

Strategy # 28: Forget Neutrality – according to Shapiro, attempting to keep your emotions under control usually backfires. The other individual can read and sense your frustration and anger in you wrinkled forehead, tense mouth, and tone. Take note that negative emotions always ruin negotiations. Rather, implore the situation to establish the positive emotions that can be conveyed during the process, such as letting a spouse who has defaulted on his part of responsibilities know that you appreciate and admire his/her hard work and the extra cash he is earning.

Power Negotiation - Getting To The YES

STRATEGY #18: Know the right time to close a discussion

If the other party is about to close the deal, your role is to make it easy for them to put into actions whatever aspects of negotiation happened.

STRATEGY #19: Always be prepared

An effective negotiation won't work if you're not prepared, plus you're becoming aggressive for the wrongful reasons.

STRATEGY #20: Consider the objectives from other parties involved

Negotiations can be stemmed by emotional motivations depending on what both parties agreed. That being said, you need to consider more the objective side of what you're talking about, instead of going through their emotions in order to make a deal successfully.

STRATEGY #21: If the other party created a first proposal/offer, set parameters in your negotiation

Allow yourself to gauge your response and set parameters while negotiating to your advantage. Although some experts suggested that your proposal should be on the first one on the table, this strategy will let other parties be in favor of you.

STRATEGY #22: Plan your flow of proposals/counter-proposals

This strategy will give you more room to negotiate.

ground, making good compliments and talking about your mutual interests

Talk about something you're both into before starting to ask for what you want. The best way to achieve this is by approaching the other party talking about an impartial topic of shared interest, such as knitting or baseball. This assists both parties to relax and begin the conversation flow. Shift to the issue at stake by saying, "I would like to talk about a certain issue crucial to me, but I would first want to hear your side of it."

STRATEGY #15: Don't take your negotiations personally

Maybe getting what you want will bring out the best in you, but you won't be able to establish good relations with others because you're taking the negotiations personally. When the other party says something that is somewhat objective, do not create arguments. You can counteract what they said by coming up with your own suggestions. Personal attack against the other party is a big no!

STRATEGY #16: Show respect to people

In negotiating, no discount is worth jeopardizing relationships, burning bridges or simply making others feel disrespected. Give respect and you'll get respect.

STRATEGY #17: Walk away for good reasons

In some cases of negotiation, there are things you're not comfortable hearing or saying, thus you make it to a point of walking away. According to experts, it's excusable to walk away if you have reasons that other parties will understand.

· · ·

STRATEGY #10: Offering an ultimatum is a big no!

Get rid of words such as "I demand 30% off, otherwise I won't buy anymore!", "Take it or leave it" or "This is my final offer." Remember, nobody likes being told by others what to do.

STRATEGY #11: Don't be too vague

Stop going around the bush in tiptoeing your ways to make the negotiation complicated. Instead of insinuating over what you want and expecting too much from other parties, ask for your desired outcome with clarity.

Strategy #12Listen First – a common saying among the negotiators says that whoever speaks the most during the process negotiation loses. According to Bobby Covic, the author of 'Everything is Negotiable!' Becoming the first person to listen is vital to establishing trust. Just getting right the listening segment of a negotiation can satisfy many parties of the principal concerns. Nevertheless, actually paying attention (listening) to what the opposing party is saying is difficult.

STRATEGY #13: Talk less, listen more

You don't need to talk a lot when negotiating. A person who talks more usually ends up with regrets. Silence makes some people feel awkward – true! But less talk means fewer mistakes – and we don't want that to happen while negotiating, right?

STRATEGY #14: Start negotiating by finding a common

Strategy #6: Use other parties' names

This is a basic strategy which seems to be forgotten by everyone else. Using other parties' names will not cause dispute between you and certain individuals for as long as you seek permission, and make sure that there aren't any conflicts going on.

Strategy #7: Don't be afraid to ask "open-ended" questions

Few examples of open-ended questions are "What can we do with the discount?" or "What is it for?" Open-ended questions require detailed explanation, so it's not answerable by "Yes" or "No". A negotiation isn't effective if you keep on answering yes or no without further explanations.

Strategy #8: Seek for alternative options

Many places have secondary options, reduced rates and all types of discounts or alternatives that are applicable. In some cases, you'll never know which particular option exists unless you'll ask. In negotiations, there are always more than two ways to remedy a solution.

Strategy #9: Demand for what you want

The world is a better place for awesome people – true! However, most of them get too busy with their jobs just to figure out what they want for others (and themselves). People are demanding for help, so you need to show them what to do and they'll also do the same for you.

. . .

Power Negotiation - Getting To The YES

Negotiating can be fun and stressful. Sometimes, you may not probably like this idea. However, keep in mind that without negotiating, you won't be able to create a positive outcome in your decisions.

Actually, we all negotiate whether we like it or not. If you ignore it, then you'll come out a loser. Quite a number of people try to put up an outcome that may be harmful to others, but these people only do what is good for their interest.

STRATEGY #3: **Explore new things**

If negotiation makes you feel prickly or uncomfortable, focus on doing or exploring things that are out of your comfort zone. You don't need to become a perfect negotiator to achieve the desired results.

STRATEGY #4: **Find someone who can help you out**

In negotiating, take note that the first person you'll approach isn't always there to deal with every situation. If they don't have the time to make changes in your negotiation, then approach others politely.

STRATEGY #5: **Never dismiss someone with a bad note**

If you need to consider other parties, don't forget to remind the person/s you're currently negotiating with. Tell them that you're happy, and you appreciate their services. Of course, don't forget to state your reasons why you need to consider other parties to avoid confrontation.

. . .

implemented in phases. Parties may be very willing to contract with a rival in the event an opportunity presents itself to show that each party is honoring its pledges along the way. As soon as the trust is destroyed, how can parties recuperate? One of the ways for a party that has lost his/her integrity with the other party because of past bad-faith actions is through gestures, as a way to compensate for previous grievances. For instance, the party that failed to pay on a contractual responsibility may have to make advance payments on a novel contract so as to persuade a poorly treated party that they are worth conducting future business with.

Key Strategies (Ways) on How to Become an Effective Negotiator

A "MORE NATURAL" approach to negotiation brought success to many individuals and groups. Here, you don't make a fuss, burn bridges and force your way into situations. A natural way of negotiating is equivalent to an effective way of doing it. But the question is how does it work? In this chapter we'll discuss 21 strategies on how to become effective in negotiating.

STRATEGY #1: **Be aware of what you're willing to accept**

Not all negotiations are planned ahead of time. Nonetheless, you can get rid of a stupid mistake by knowing where/when you're going to accept things or call it quits before starting your negotiations.

STRATEGY #2: **Accept the fact that negotiating is essential**

Power Negotiation - Getting To The YES

ests. Finally, agreements that are settled this way may prove difficult to employ if both sides later determine that the arrangement called for an answer without legality. Nevertheless, there is a much better way to handle the process of negotiation. This includes invoking unbiased criteria into the process of negotiation.

COMMITMENTS

AN AGREEMENT IS ONLY LASTING if all parties to the contract honor the pledges that they make. On the other hand, those that do not uphold their promises will be subjected to the other party's resentment, suffer loss of integrity, and risk losing the other party in the negotiations. Even those outside the deal (in the event that a word about their reputation goes public) will decline to enter into any future deal with them.

THEREFORE, it is advisable that no side of the negotiation should deliberately create pledges that they don't expect to honor. According to Fisher and Ertel, during the process of negotiating, the parties ought to think wisely about the type of commitments they ought to be ready to make. Can they honor them? When will every party be anticipated to uphold on their promises? How far-reaching should a commitment be?

ACCORDING TO VARIOUS RESEARCHERS, one way to establish trust is to build a commitment structure capable of being hindered by common communication incompetence and blunders. For instance, parties may only focus on their own reactions and forget to pay attention to what the second party to the negotiation is saying. Listening offers vital information of the other party and exhibits that you are concentrating to the other party's thoughts and deferential of their concerns.

FISHER AND URY advocate for active listening as a way to enhance communication skills. This infers listening "not to articulate a reaction, but to appreciate the second party as they appreciate themselves. Paraphrasing without actually agreeing, constantly conceding to what is or not said, and asking questions are great ways to show that you are attentive or actively listening.

CRITERIA OR LEGITIMACY

WHEN NEGOTIATING OVER A STAND, parties to the negotiation create a state of affairs wherein one side has to compromise his original claim for the negotiations bargain to be successful. Positional bargaining is negotiating wherein two parties lock into discordant positions. This can result in a competition of wills, deadlock, and bitterness. They uphold that when the parties approach negotiations in this manner, even when coming to an agreement, it may be at a very high cost. For instance, positional bargainers may lastly come to an agreement that seems to "divide the differences" amid their two opinions, although a more sensibly composed answer would have been appropriate for both parties inter-

Power Negotiation - Getting To The YES

As indicated in theorange story, when two entities (companies, nations, and individuals) get stuck into routine patterns of thinking or solutions, they quickly become shadowed to the likelihoods that a bit of creative thinking might disclose. Since the process of recognizing options, or probable solutions to an issue, encourages creative thinking and increases problem-solving aptitudes, it is as vital to the process as identifying fundamental interests. Creating options through techniques like brainstorming, a method that involves asking all parties to note any new idea without dismissing or criticizing those concepts, helps to inspire creative thinking of an issue and boosts the odds that the involved parties will develop a "win-win" solution.

COMMUNICATION

FISHER AND URI noted in their research studies that for negotiation to take place, communication has to occur. Similarly, feeling heard is a significant interest for the parties in a negotiation. Excellent communication skills can modify attitudes, overcome or prevent misunderstanding and deadlock help to enhance relationships. Furthermore, good communication skills are vital to persuasively communicate your message, and also to precisely comprehend the other party's message.

ADDITIONALLY, integrative approaches emphasize the significance of information sharing as a way of revealing interests and assisting parties to establish common threats or problems. Nonetheless, the roles of negotiators are often

ALTERNATIVES

TO SET REALISTIC TARGET, negotiators are advised to begin by considering some important questions, such as where both sides will be when they don't come to an agreement and what other solutions they have for achieving their goals if they can't count on the other party' cooperation. As earlier mentioned, attention to substitutes is a vital aspect of integrative and distributive-based approaches. Nevertheless, contrary to the stress placed on concepts like bottom lines and reservation points in positional approaches to negotiating, integrative approaches appear to take a bit more nuanced outlook on the role of substitutes in negotiation. This, according to various researchers, is vital for both the parties to be aware of their BATNA - Best Alternative to a Negotiated Agreement - before and throughout the negotiation phases.

IDENTIFYING the options

AS SOON AS the parties have started building relationships and exchanging information so as to get a much clear comprehension of the interests in the balance, the parties ought to resort to the task of producing alternatives. In negotiations, preferences are feasible solutions to problems shared by at least two parties. In integrative negotiations, options represent probable methods of attaining as much interest as possible for both parties.

. . .

researchers, parties in dispute usually forget that the other side has people who like them, are prone to human frailties like mistaken assumptions, emotions, and potential for misunderstanding, in trying to achieve their goals. Hence, it's vital to isolate the problem from the people. This infers finding a method for solving problems devoid of getting sidetracked by individual elements, and agreeing in a way that will maintain the relationship.

THIS WAY, the parties are likely to cooperate more and comfortably share information. As a result, the prospects of the parties arriving at a win-win outcome are high. To build good relationships, the parties are advised to consider using tactics that can help them know each other better. This may include staying on after official negotiations, finding means to meet informally, and arriving in time to chat.

IN ADDITION, negotiators should remain aware of vital strategies and considerations to help them feel as like they can come out of the negotiation with dignity, and a good view of the other party. This may infer taking steps to ensure that neither participant is compelled to appear personally compromised or lose face as a result of having tolerated the demands of the other party. Alternatively, negotiators ought to know that protecting their dignity should not be key to the negotiation that it clouds the significance of the important issues, or generate deep conflicts that can prevent or delay progress toward an agreement.

.   .   .

PRACTICAL STEPS TO INCORPORATE BARGAINING: The 7 elements of principled negotiation

IDENTIFYING interests

ACCORDING TO URY AND FISHER, the first phase of principled negotiations is identifying the interests involved in the problem area rather than dealing with the negotiating parties' positions. This distinction is vital in the integrative school. Stands or positions signify the specified objectives and stances of the parties in the negotiation and are the heart of distributive bargaining, while interests are the basic reasons that explain individual stands.

INTEGRATIVE APPROACHES UPHOLD that to effectively negotiate, the parties must go beyond stands and look to satisfy true essential interests. This way, negotiators can tackle issues of common concern with greater understanding, flexibility, and creativity. Interests may be difficult to identify compared to positions and can go unspoken or even concealed behind a party's declared position or demand. Normally, participants may not have prudently defined their own fundamental interests.

PEOPLE

THIS IS THE SECOND ELEMENT. According to various

6

TYPES OF NEGOTIATORS

Researchers from the Harvard University Negotiation Project identified these three types of negotiators:

1. Principled – These are negotiators who bargain integrative solutions by "side-stepping" their commitment in negotiating with specific positions. In other words, principled negotiators focus on the problem than the needs, motives and intentions of other parties involved.

2. Hard – These negotiators often use strategies to utilize or influence phrases commonly used in negotiating ("Either you take it or leave it", "This is our final offer" etc.). Sometimes, the hard type of negotiators insists on their position, and is distrustful of other parties.

3. Soft – These negotiators are the total opposite of the hard ones. The offers they create aren't just for their own interests, but also for other parties. Soft negotiators yield to the demands of others in order to preserve good relations with fellow negotiators and avoid confrontation.

. . .

Integrative negotiations (win / win) – negotiations are said to be integrative when the party's interest and aspirations are respected, regardless of where they come from. It is built on mutual respect and tolerance for diverse opinion and objective.

The benefits of this form of negotiation are those which realize better, more viable solutions, parties feel better, and their relationships improve. Both support the arrangements solutions and they both win. This form of negotiation develops, saves and reinforces long-term business associations.

This negotiation's optical evades conflict positions. The negotiation environment is characterized by optimism and confidence, and the arrangement, once realized, can be appreciated. Specific tactics are built on shared concessions (for instance, shorter terms of delivery for an instant payment).

Rational negotiation – in this form of negotiation, the parties don't have one particular objective or to obtain consent of both parties, but also to try resolve differences in a neutral position rather than either of their position. For this to be attained there ought to be clearly defined shared interests in a complete transparent sincerity, devoid of any recourse to suspicion or conceal.

It starts with identification of the problems that require being solved, as solutions to questions such as: How is it exhibited? What's wrong? What are the conflicting facts to the situation? Where is evil? It proceeds with a situation diagnosis, focusing on the problem averting causes. Then theoretical solutions are looked for and agreed upon regarding the actions from which some may be employed.

5

TYPES OF NEGOTIATIONS

Business negotiation – this is a particular type of negotiation, focused on the presence of a service or product on one part and a want to gratify, on the other part. The contract is commercial and can be used in a sale contract (leasing, partnership, etc.), a command, a convention, an act of commerce, or simply alter certain clauses of price range, quality or conditions of transport, delivery, etc.

Distributive negotiation – it is a form of negotiation whereby one party either / or, choses between winning and losing. It takes a transaction form where for one party to win, the other one must lose. Every partner's approval comes at the grantor's expense and vice versa.

Here, negotiation bring the two parties with opposing interests face to face and becomes a conflict of forces where one side has to win. Any consent is believed to be a symbol of weakness, while every effective attack is a symbol of power. The objective of the negotiation(s) will be an arrangement that won't consider the other party's interests and in fact, it will be better if the consequence hit hardest.

ested or simply don't like to be negotiated unless they're warranted. During negotiation, avoiders often dodge its provoking aspect, and are perceived by many as subtle and tactful.

- **Accommodating** – This involves individuals who are already used to solving other parties' problems. Accommodators are deemed sensitive towards body language, verbal signs, and emotional states of other parties.

4

NEGOTIATING STYLES

Self-help expert R.G Shell identified these five negotiating styles in his recent study. Each style varies based on the interests and context of parties.

- **Compromising** - This is done by individuals (or groups) who are too eager to close deals that are equal (or fair) for all parties involved in the entire negotiation. Compromisers are very useful when there isn't enough time in completing the deal.

- **Competing** – This is done by individuals enjoying negotiations because it gives them the opportunity to achieve something. Competitive negotiators are said to have the strongest instincts for negotiating in almost all aspects. On the other hand, they usually neglect the importance of "party-based" relationships.

- **Collaborating** – This generally involves individuals enjoying negotiations highlighted by solving difficult problems in creative ways.

- Contrary to competitors, collaborators are good in understanding the concerns and interests of parties.

- **Avoiding** – This involves individuals who aren't inter-

THESE APPROACHES sharply contrast distributive approaches of frame negotiations as relations with win-win possibility. While a zero-sum outlook sees the objective of the negotiations as a determination to demand one's portion over a "limited amount of pie", these (integrative) strategies and theories seek ways of 'expanding the pie' or creating value to ensure there is enough for both parties to share from the negotiation. These approaches utilize objective criteria, seek to develop conditions of common gain, and highlight the significance of exchanging data amongst participants and group problem-solving. Since integrative approaches focus on cooperation, mutual gains, problem solving, and joint decision-making, integrative strategies encourage parties to collaborate to develop win-win solutions. This involves searching for shared goals, uncovering interests, and generating options.

NEGOTIATORS MAY SEEK ways to build value, and develop common values as a basis of making decisions regarding how outputs ought to be claimed and the person to claim them. This approach to negotiations is based on social decision-making, political theory, research on labor disputes, and international relations.

Power Negotiation - Getting To The YES

attitudes, and trust in the negotiated results. Other researchers have emphasized factors like expectation, relationships, skills, trust, culture, norms, and attitudes.

CONCESSION EXCHANGE (Processual) approach

THIS APPROACH SHARES the features of both strategic approach (results) and structural approach (power). Nevertheless, they define a different form of mechanism that focuses on learning. Zartman believes this approach (processual approach) considers negotiation 'a learning process' whereby parties respond to one another concession behavior. According this viewpoint negotiation comprise a chain of concessions that mark every stage in the negotiation. Both parties used them to signify their intentions and to inspire movement in the position of their opponent. Both parties "utilize their bids to react to the earlier counteroffer and to impact the subsequent one; these offers are an exercise in power.

THE RISKS here that the parties participating in concession-trading may fail to recognize prospects to find new, shared beneficial answers to their mutual dilemma and instead end-up in an entirely regressive process that leaves them both with fewer gains compared to what they could have gained if they had chosen a more creative tactic.

INTEGRATIVE APPROACH

. . .

CRITICAL RISK MODEL **of crisis bargaining** by Ellsberg - like the game theory, it utilizes basic utility numbers to elucidate decision-making behavior. However, it introduces the perception that the parties utilize probability estimations when making sensible calculations as to whether to concede or not concede, or stand strong in disaster negotiation.

BEHAVIORAL APPROACH

IT EMPHASIZES the role played by individual characteristics or negotiators' personalities in determining the way and result of negotiated arrangements. Behavioral models may describe negotiations as interactions among personality 'types' that usually take dichotomies forms, such as headliners, or soft liners or warriors and shopkeepers where negotiators are depicted as either diplomatically conceding to the other party's demands to maintain peace or ruthlessly fighting for all.

THIS APPROACH STEMS from experimental and psychological traditions, and also from centuries-old diplomatic agreements. These traditions believe in the notion that negotiations, whether amid employers, unions, and nations, or neighbors are totally about the persons involved. Whereas the game theory depends on the presumption that the parties to the negotiation 'game' are uniformly rational, payoff maximizing, and featureless bodies, the behavioral approach focus on human skills, emotions, and tendencies. They may also highlight the roles played by the 'arts' of personality, perception, persuasion, individual motivation,

Power Negotiation - Getting To The YES

biology. While the structural approaches focus on the functions of means (like power) in negotiations, strategic models emphasize on the end part of ends (objectives) in determining results. These models are also of rational decision. Negotiators are considered rational choice makers with identified substitutes who make decisions guided by their evaluation of the option that will maximize their gains or ends, often termed as 'payoffs'. Actors pick from a set of choices of probable actions to try and realize the desired results. Every actor has an exceptional 'incentive structure' that consists of a range of costs linked to the diverse actions pooled together with a range of prospects that reveal the livelihoods of diverse actions resulting in the preferred results.

THESE APPROACHES ARE normative in nature. Since they are rooted in the conviction that there is a single ultimate solution to all negotiation problems, they strive to signify "what ultra-smart, perfectly rational, super-humans ought to do in competitive, interactive situations, such as bargains. As they seek the 'best answers' from all angles of a negotiation. This is referred to as Symmetrically Prescriptive. The strategic approaches are the bases for negotiation models like critical risk theory and game theory.

GAME THEORY – it uses recognized mathematical models to define, predict, or recommend the actions that the parties should take to maximize their individual gains when the outcome of any choice they make will rely on the choices made by a different actor.

.   .   .

outcome of the structural features or characteristics that describe each individual negotiation. These features may include characteristics like the composition (whether every side comprises various groups or is monolithic) or relative strength of the rival parties, and the issues and the number of parties participating in the negotiations. These approaches find clarifications of results in patterns of relations between the parties or their objectives.

In structural approaches, analysts tend to describe negotiations as engagement scenarios between rivals who maintain discordant goals. Analysts who implement a structural approach in their studies share an emphasis on the resources parties offer to a negotiation.

NEVERTHELESS, structural approaches have their limitations. According to critics, structural explanations seem to highlight the function of power, and specifically on difficult aspects of power. In addition, structural approaches emphasize on taking positions. However, the negotiators ought to be cognizant that blind attachment to gaining the most from a negotiation irrespective of the resultant satisfaction of other participants, can be a bad lasting strategy if it infers that the other party will lose its ability or will to keep his/her side of the contract.

STRATEGIC APPROACH

STRATEGIC APPROACHES HAVE a base in mathematics, rational choice theory and decision theory, and also gain from major additions from the fields of conflict analysis, economics, and

3
AN OVERVIEW OF NEGOTIATION
APPROACHES

Theorists contrast on the question regarding how to classify the leading school of thoughts on negotiation. For instance Daniel Druckman describes the leading schools of thought on negotiation theory as conforming to four tactics to negotiation. Negotiation as: diplomatic politics, puzzle solving, organizational management, and a bargaining game. On the other hand, Howard Raiffa suggests a number of 'approaches' designed around the scopes of prescription-description and symmetry-asymmetry.

This overview of schools of thought or negotiation approaches presented here is founded on a summary provided by William Zartman, researcher, theorist, and practitioner on negotiations. It consists of five diverse core approaches or levels of analysis. They include the structural, the processual (commonly known as 'concession-exchange), the strategic, the integrative, and the behavioral approaches.

Structural approaches
These approaches consider negotiated results to be an

2

THE BASICS OF EFFECTIVE
NEGOTIATION STRATEGIES

Negotiation usually occurs in legal proceedings, government agencies, non-profit groups and businesses. Negotiation theory is a study often practiced by professional negotiators since this involves various partnership deals with brokers, legislators, diplomats, multinational company owners, and other parties.

Negotiating Tactics

There are various ways in categorizing the basic elements of negotiation. One view of negotiating is covered by three main elements: process, substance and behavior. These elements vary depending on the parties involved. The process has something to do with how one party negotiates with another. The behavior and Substance, meanwhile, have something to do with the relationship between two parties and the agenda of their negotiation, respectively.

Other basic elements of negotiation are tactics, tools, process and strategy.

Power Negotiation - Getting To The YES

party when it is no longer be avoided so as to soothe the other party for a little bit longer.

WHAT MAKES NEGOTIATED SOLUTIONS POSSIBLE?

THE VARIOUS KEY concepts utilized in both integrative and distributive approaches to negotiations will help us answer this question. In any negotiation, every party has a 'bottom line' or reservation point. It is a level beyond which a participant won't go, and would rather ends negotiations. Additionally, it is a point that is generally not known by other participants and a value that according to Raiffa and others ought to be left secret. The bottom line of negotiating parties assists to frame the prospects and an agreement's possible scope. For instance:

RESERVATION POINTS OVERLAP: A sweet deal

A LOCAL MILK producer and his chief milk supplier are negotiating a new contract. Although the producer hopes to pay less, she is aware that still the purchase would be worth at a maximum price of 10€/liter. Here, 10€/liter is the producer's reservation point. The supplier is aware of that (but still hopes the negotiations will get him a higher price) he would agree to sell his stock of raw milk to the producer at a minimum of 10€/liter. This is his reservation price given that below this value he will not agree to a deal.

THIS APPROACH CONTRADICTS approaches that aim at using negotiations as a means to increase the pie; that is, to multiply benefits to the advantage of both parties. Consequently, these approaches have a tendency to to prompt strategies that are of predatorily nature or distributive.

DISTRIBUTIVE STRATEGIES, also referred to as 'zero-sum', 'win-lose', or competitive strategies are founded on this competitive outlook of negotiations. These strategies are designed to obtain the biggest possible slice of the pie for one party (also known as 'claiming value'), whilst leaving the other party with the smallest piece possible.

HENCE, the tactics employed in this case are meant to assist those who utilize them to claim value, whereas defending against the opponent's efforts to perform the same. Given that competitive strategies yield win-lose outcomes, most people (especially those that attribute to the integrative school) consider such strategies destructive. For instance:

COERCION: refers using force, or threatening to use of force to obtain consent from the second party.

OPENING STRONG: beginning with a position higher than you genuinely estimate you can attain.

SALAMI TACTICS: lengthening a negotiation to an extremely slow pace, and only issuing a tiny concession to the second

Power Negotiation - Getting To The YES 3

NEGOTIATION IS A DIALOGUE BETWEEN TWO, three or more parties which is intended to reach a resolved point of divergence or understanding. It also refers to a method of producing an agreement via courses of action to bargain for advantage – individually and/or collectively.

A strategy on the other hand, is "a well thought out plan or method for realizing a goal." While using Tactics denotes the skill of utilizing the available resources to reach an end.

THIS GENERALLY PERTAINS TO NEGOTIATIONS. Nevertheless, note that in some situations a devious participant may enter a negotiation to satisfy some other intention, such as gaining political advantage by simply being seen to be involved in a negotiating process (regardless of whether it succeeds or not) or stalling, instead of reaching an agreement. Nevertheless, even in such instances deals may at times be made due to the dynamics that the negotiations introduce.

PROCESS ORIENTED, structural, and strategic approaches to negotiation seem to have a mutual distributive comprehension of negotiations. The above approaches involve the presumption that negotiations are no cost transactions. That is, negotiators consider negotiations contests over a fixed or limited amount of some equally desired benefit in that one party's gain is another party's loss. The entirety of available gains is usually represented figuratively as a 'pie'. Due to negotiators competition over a limited amount of some benefit or good, negotiators are optimistic of winning a 'slice' or portion of the pie at the other party's expense.

. . .

definitions of negotiation differ, theorists consent to certain basic views. Firstly, the supposition that negotiating parties agree in one or more essential respect. They both believe that their individual objectives will be served better by negotiating with the second party. Discreetly then, the negotiating parties have for a moment concluded that they might be capable of satisfying their personal concerns or objectives well, by agreeing to a solution with the second party, than by trying to satisfy their concerns or objectives individually. It is this shared perception that result in the beginning of negotiations and give up the existing dependence between the negotiating parties. This shared interest in a joint agreement is the onset of the "mutual dependence and shared interest that can exist amid participants in an encounter with which, according to Schelling (1960) "negotiation is concerned".

Basic concepts of negotiation

Strategies and Tactics

Before discussing the several approaches to negotiation, it is vital to understand the meaning of negotiation and discuss the strategies and tactics to successful negotiations and how they apply to various schools.

What is a negotiation?

. . .

1

NEGOTIATION THEORY: FOUNDATIONS & APPROACHES

Negotiation theories may be descriptive, normative, and prescriptive in nature. In addition, practitioners and theorists from a number of disciplines have established and used various levels of analysis or approaches to enhance their understanding of certain negotiation aspects. The resulting models are varied, and often highlight elements that reflect leading concerns from the disciplines' perspective from which they developed. It is not surprising then, that the official meaning of negotiation reflect the various aspects of the disciplinary, functional, and conceptual origins of the models created to explain it.

Noted negotiator and statesman Henry Kissinger described negotiation as, "a technique of merging incompatible positions into one mutual position, under a unanimity decision rule". In other research studies, theorists have depicted negotiations as events of weighted interaction between different types of personality or sensible decision-making process, diplomatic artistry, and mechanical mirror images of relative power. Although the official

INTRODUCTION

Negotiation is hands-down one of the most important skills that you can have when it comes to effectively communicating with people and making what *you* want crystal clear so that it shines like a gleaming diamond in a room. Simply, imagine walking into a room and having the ability to take over any situation that involves negotiation because of your powerful negotiating strategies and persuasion skills. This is what Power Negotiation is about – once you read and understand the masterful strategies and tips layered throughout this book you will have the ability to get *what* you want *when* you want it.

You will soon discover tips and strategies that completely reveal how to create a negotiation so that the favors are in your odds and create a winning perspective, with complete fairness. You will be guided through various ways of communicating and be shown the ways to maximize your communication strategies.

Let's get started!

CONTENTS

Introduction	v
1. Negotiation Theory: Foundations & Approaches	1
2. The Basics of Effective Negotiation Strategies	6
3. An Overview of Negotiation Approaches	7
4. Negotiating Styles	13
5. Types of Negotiations	15
6. Types of Negotiators	17
7. The Intricacies and Components of a Negotiation	32
8. Understanding How to Use Perception to Your Advantage	35
9. Why Communication is Still Key and Methods to Improve Yours?	37
10. Emotional Awareness	43
11. Closing the Gap Between Parties	45
12. Tips for Successful Negotiation	49
Afterword	55

I0252158

POWER NEGOTIATION - GETTING TO THE YES

STRATEGIES TO GET WHAT YOU WANT,
WHEN YOU WANT IT

PATRICK KENNEDY